DEVELOPMENT PROGRAMME IN PROJECT MANAGEMENT

DEVELOPMENT PROGRAMME IN PROJECT MANAGEMENT

Dr. Kumari Jyotsna

KALPAZ

First Published, 2019

Published by

Kalpaz Publications
C-30, Satyawati Nagar,
Delhi – 110052
Ph.: 011-47034999, 9811692060
www.kalpazpublications.com
E-mail: kalpaz@hotmail.com

Printed at: G. Print Process, Delhi

Cataloging in Publication Data—DK

Courtesy: D.K. Agencies (P) Ltd. <docinfo@dkagencies.com>

Kumari Jyotsna, *Dr.*, **author.**

Development programme in project management / Dr. Kumari Jyotsna.

pages cm

ISBN 9789353240714

1. Project management. I. Title.

LCC HD69.P75K86 2019 | DDC 658.404 23

Contents

Preface 7
1. Concept and Definition of Project Management 9
2. Planning and Analysis of Project 15
3. Project Finance 29
4. Project Appraisal 33
5. Project Organisation and Contract Management 39
6. Project Implementation 47

Preface

To be very precise, a project is a specific activity on which money is spent on the expectation of returns. There is therefore, a specific starting point, a specific end point & is intended to achieve a specific objective.

Every project has three basic attributes: the input characteristics, output characteristics & the social benefit characteristics. Precisely, project Management covers the entire gamut of project.

Project Management is receiving much attention these days. Almost every day newspapers carry advertisement asking for project Mangers. The scenario was not so bright a few years ago. For that matter even today, though lots of seminars are held on Project Management, hardly any university offers degree course to students to formally qualify as project managers. Thus while there is a demand, there is a little supply and this has created all sorts of problems.

Project Management demands a judicious mix of science, arts & politics. It is therefore understood that projecting the pure form or the scientific aspect of project Management as a panacea for all the ills that plague a project will be extremely impractical. However, this book intends to deal with the scientific aspect of Development programme in Project Management in detail because that alone can be taught easily and applied uniformly. The art & politics of Management will vary from place to place, country to country & will depend on the concerned individuals & organizations.

This book has been divided in to six chapters:-

1. Concept and definition of Project Management
2. Planning & analysis of project.
3. Project finance
4. Project appraisal

5. Project organization & contract Management
6. Project implementation.

All chapters have been organized in sequence in which a project is managed. Project Management is an approach that assures results and for those who are interested in results, this book attempts to show how to apply "Development programme in Project Management" to their project & obtain results.

This book has been written with the intention of bridging the gap between theory & practice and, therefore, if it promotes further thought & action in this direction, I will consider my efforts amply rewarded.

I look forward to receiving suggestions from students, entrepreneurs, managers & readers for improving the contents & presentation of this book.

No book can be written without the support of others who have produced similar works. In acknowledging the contributions of my seniors & Colleagues for creation of this book, I must first convey my deepest thanks & sense of gratitude to chairman S.N. Sinha Institute of Business Management, Prof. N.P. Singh, for his ungrudging help at all stages. I would also like to extend my sincere thanks to Prof. P.S. Tomar HOD Management for his suggestions for effecting a number of stylistic improvements in preparation & giving final shape to the book.

Lastly I wish to extend my sincere thanks to my husband Prof. Sudhir Kumar for his help and guidance in preparing the manuscript. I reserve my deepest thanks to my son & daughter for their co-operation and not disturbing me in completion of this voluminous work.

Dr. Kumari Jyotsna

1

Concept and Definition of Project Management

1. Concept and Definition of Project Management

1.1 Concept and Definition

In the business scenario, an Organization (Public or Private) has to grow. Growth is necessary for at least survival. An organization therefore makes a corporate plan. As a part of the Corporate Plan, an organization makes different strategies for growth. Different strategies give rise to different projects like Modernization, Diversification, Expansion, etc.

Similarly, a Government, for the sake of growth of the country, takes up different developmental projects. Infrastructural development is given top priority by the State and Central Government. Golden Quadrilateral road project connecting the four metros is one such example.

A project is started to achieve a specific objective. A project is completed as soon as the objective is fulfilled. The project lives in between two cut-off points and the time spent is known as project life cycle.

A project has been defined by a Project Management Institute of USA as 'a combination of human and non-human resources pooled together in a temporary organization to achieve a specific purpose'.

1.2 Characteristic Features of project

2. Objective – A project has a fixed set of objectives.
3. A project is one entity and is normally entrusted with one responsibility.
4. Team work – A project calls for a team work.

5. Change – A project sees many changes throughout its life.
6. Uniqueness – No two projects are exactly similar
7. Made to Order – A project is always made to order of its customer
8. High level of sub-contracting – Normally, majority of work in a project is done through contractor.
9. Risk and Uncertainty – Every project has the risk and uncertainty associated with it. The degree of risk and uncertainty will depend on how it has been formulated.
10. Life-Cycle – A project has a life cycle represented by:
    (a) Conception phase
    (b) Definition phase
    (c) Planning and Organizing phase
    (d) Implementation phase
    (e) Project cleanup phase

1.2 Project Classification

(a) Project of different sectors – Project for PSUs

(b) Industrial and non-Industrial Projects

Non-Industrial Projects

- Health Care, Public Education, etc.

Industrial Projects

- Projects belonging to industrial organizations

(c.) Projects belonging to core sectors

Complex mega Projects by Government

-Power Projects, Ports, Highways, Mining, Steel

(d.) Need based Projects

Projects growing out of corporate plans

Balancing, Expansion, Modernization, Replacement, Diversification

Another way of Classifying

- Green Field Projects
- Brown Field Projects

Green Field Projects - Completely new project, started from scratch. For example, someone starting a new factory on a land acquired for the purpose. In case of diversification also, when new products are to be produced, it can be a green field project.

Brown Field Project - A project implemented in the premises of a working plant is known as Brown Field Project. Modernization, Replacement projects come under this.

Idea Generation for New Projects

1.3.1 Analysis of the input and output of existing industries

1.3.2 Analysis of the performance of existing industries

1.3.3 Examine exports and imports

1.3.4 Suggestion of Financial Institutions and development agencies

1.3.5 Survey of local resources

1.3.6 Government's guidelines

1.3.7 New Technologies

1.3.8 Emulating consumption pattern from abroad

1.3.9 Restoring life to sick units

1.3.10 Analysis of unsatisfied needs of consumers, identifying the deficiencies which can be satisfied.

1.3.11 International and national trade fairs and industry exhibition

1.3.12 Stimulate creativity for generating new project idea by any of the Following lines:

- Modification
- Rearrangement
- Magnification
- Reduction
- Substitution
- Combination, etc.

1.3.13 Change factor

1.3.14 Initial selection of project ideas - Screening

1. Match with entrepreneur's interest, personality and resources
2. Fit with national interest
3. Availability of inputs
4. Adequacy of market
5. Reasonableness of cost
6. Acceptability of risk level

1.4 Project Life Cycle Phases

All projects have to pass through the following phases:

1. Conception phase
2. Definition phase

3. Planning and Organization phase
4. Implementation phase
5. Project cleanup phase

1.4.1 Conception Phase

This is the phase during which the project idea germinates. The idea may first come to the mind when one is seriously trying to overcome certain problems. Thos idea needs to be examined in the light of objectives and constraints and what finally becomes acceptable may form the future project.

1.4.2 Definition Phase

The definition phase of the project will develop the idea generates during conception phase and produces a document describing the project in sufficient detail covering all aspects that are necessary for the customs and/or financial institutions to make up their minds on the project idea.

The areas to be examined during this phase, say a cement plant, may be as follows:

1. Raw material – qualitative and quantitative evaluation of raw material like lime stone.
2. Plant's size/capacity
3. Location and site
4. Technology/process selection - selection of optimum technology, reasons for selection and description of the selected technologies.
5. Project layout
6. Plant and Machinery - Selection of optimum equipment, reasons for selection, description of selected equipment and machineries, stating number, types, specification, capacity, source and company.
7. Electrical and instrumentation works
8. Civil engineering works
9. Utilities - Power and water
10. Manpower and organizational pattern
11. Financial analysis - Total investment
    - Cost, sources of finance, total production costs and evaluation of financial viability.
12. Implementation schedule

1.4.3 Planning and Organizing Phase

This phase can effectively start only after definition phase but, in practice, it starts much earlier, almost immediately after conception phase. Following are dealt with during this phase:

1. Project infrastructure and enabling services
2. System design and basic engineering package
3. Organization and manpower
4. Schedules and budgets
5. Licensing and governmental clearance
6. Finance
7. Systems and procedure
8. Identification of project manager
9. Design basis, general conditions for purchase and contracts
10. Site preparation and investigation
11. Construction resource and material
12. Work packaging

1.4.3 Implementation Phase

This is the period of hectic activity for the project. During this period, something that starts growing in the field and people, for the first time, can see the project. Preparation of specification of equipment and machinery, ordering of equipment, lining up of construction contractors, issue of construction of equipment, foundation, equipment and machinery erection, plant electrical, piping, instrumentation, testing, checking, trial run and commissioning take place during this phase. As far as 80-85% of project work is done in this phase.

1.4.4 Project Cleanup Phase

This is a transition phase in which hardware built with active involvement of various agencies is physically handed over for production to a different agency who was not so involved earlier. Drawing, documents, files, operation and maintenance manuals are catalogued and handed over to the customer. Test runs are done to the satisfaction of customers. Any change required at the last minute for fulfillment of contractual obligations in respect of performance has, therefore, to be completed during this phase to the satisfaction of the customer. Project accounts are closed, material reconciliation are carried out, outstanding payments are made and dues collected during this phase.

2

Planning and Analysis of Project

1. Project Preparation

Once a definite idea emerges as viable and compatible as per the customer's requirement, requirement, a Project Report is prepared to make an Inter-departmental study of the project idea from different angles. That report is called Project Feasibility Report. Since a detailed feasibility report takes time, a Pre-feasibility study is prepared prior to making actual Feasibility Study.

2.1 Pre-feasibility Study

This study examines the following:

(a) Market and plant's capacity
(b) Material inputs
(c) Location and site
(d) Technology and Equipment
(e) Civil Engineering Works
(f) Manpower
(g) Financial Analysis – investment cost, project financing, production cost and commercial viability.

2.2 Feasibility Study

If pre-feasibility throws up an opportunity, the Feasibility Study is taken up. This study includes:

- Market analysis
- Technical analysis

- Financial Analysis
- Social Cost Benefit Analysis
- Environment Impact Analysis

2.2.1 Market Analysis

It includes the following:

(a) Demand forecasting
(b) Estimates of demand
(c) Existing capacity
(d) Distribution
(e) Price

2.2.1.1 Demand Forecasting

Methods of Demand Forecasting

Most commonly used methods of forecasting may be grouped under two types:

(a) Qualitative methods
(b) Quantitative methods

(a) Qualitative Method - It includes:

(i) Expert Opinion – Option is taken from the experts regarding their estimates of future demand. Experts may include executives directly involved in the market such as dealers, distributors and suppliers or others whose major interest is in the forecast itself such as industry analyst, specialists, Marketing Consultants, Officers of Trade Association, etc. Each expert is asked independently to provide a confidential estimate and the results could be average.

(ii) Delphi Method: A variant of expert opinion method consists of an attempt to arrive at a consensus in an uncertain area by questioning a group of experts repeatedly until the response appears to coverage or the issues causing disagreement are clearly defined.

(iii) Survey of buyer's intention: The most direct method of estimating demand in the short run is to ask the customers what they are planning to buy for the coming time period usually a year. This method also known as opinion survey is most suitable when bulk of the sales is made to industrial producers. Here the burden of forecasting is shifted to the customer. Care should be taken about the estimate because customer often exaggerate their estimate or may be uncertain about their requirements.

(b) Quantitative Method -

(i) **Moving Averages** - Moving averages are averages that are updated as new information is received. With the moving average, a manager takes a periodic observations and average there. Then they proceed with latest observation and discard the old observations.

Days	Sales (in '000 Rs.)
1.1.04	46
2.1.04	54
3.1.04	53
4.1.04	46
5.1.04	58
6.1.04	49

Let us assume the sales manager has the following sales figure for 6 days:

$$\frac{46+54+53+46+58+49}{6}=\frac{306}{6}=51$$

By taking a 6 day moving average he can predict for 7th day 7.1.04 by simple taking average of 6 days i.e.

Now prediction for 7th day = 51
Say actual for 7th day = 54

If he wants to predict for 8th day he will discard the date for 1.1.04 – 46 and add actual of 7th day – 54.

Prediction for 8th day

$$\frac{54+53+46+58+49+54}{6}=\frac{314}{6}=52.3$$

Limitations of the method are:

1. All figures are given equal weightage
2. Once has to retain huge amount data to find the moving average

(ii) Exponential Smoothing

It is a popular forecasting technique for short run forecast. It uses a weight to the figure.

New forecast = Last periods forecast + L (Last period's actual demand – Last period's forecast)

Where L is a smoothing constant

$$0 < L < 1$$

Symbolically

F_t = Ft – 1 + L (At -1 – Ft – 1) a Ft -1 (1 – L) + Lat -1

F_t = New forecast for period 't'

Ft – 1 = Previous forecast

At – 1 = Previous periods actual demand

The higher is 'L' the higher weight is given to more recent information.

Period	Actual Sales	Forecast Sales
7	70	63.0

Forecast for period 8th day (Say L =0.2)

Ft = 63.0 + 0.2 (70 – 63) = 64.4

3. Method of Least Square :

This method provides a rigorous basis for determining linear trend. The linear relationship is choosen in such a manner that the sum of squared deviations of the observations from the line is minimized.

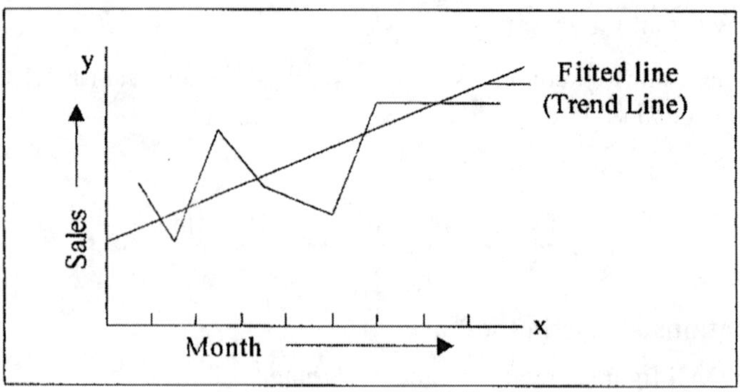

A line in the form $Y = a + bx$ is fitted by putting the value of x, y can be predicted. Then seasonal fluctuations are adjusted.

In the similar manner in some cases curves are fitted for non-linear trends.

Advantages of least square method:

(i) It uses all observations

(ii) The straight line of curve is derived by an objective and statistical procedure

(iii) A measure of goodness of fit is possible

Disadvantages (Limitations)

(i) The method is complicated

Some of other techniques

(a) Leading indicator method: Leading indicators are variables, which change ahead of other variables, the lagging variables. Hence, observed changes in leading indicators may be used to predict the changes in lagging variable. For example change in the level of urbanization (a leading indicator) may be used to predict the change in the demand for air conditioners (a lagging variable).

(b) Econometric Method: An economic model is a mathematical representation of economic relationship derived from the economic theory. The objective of the analysis is to forecast the future behavior of the economic variables incorporated in the model.

An example of relationship: $Dt = a0 + a1pt + a2Nt$
Where Dt = demand for a certain product in year t

Pt = price for the product in year t
Nt = National income for year t
A0, a1, a2 are constants.

2.2.1.2 Estimates of Demand: Based on the demand forecasting some estimates are made taking into account the existing capacity, distribution etc.

2.2.1.3 Existing Capacity: There should be assessment of existing capacity, present level of production, capacity utilization, extent of import and projected supply considering the plants under consideration.

2.2.1.4 Distribution: Covering channels of distribution, mode of transport, mode of packing and consist of distribution, Government policies, etc.

2.2.1.5 Price: Covering both domestic and international price trends, control on prices as imposed by the government prevailing duties and taxes.

2.2.2 Technical Analysis: This should include the following:

(a) Product Pattern Plant Capacity
(b) Process Selection
(c) Plant Location
(d) Machineries and equipment
(e) Man Power
(f) Structures and Civil Works
(g) Project Chart and Layouts
(h) Work Schedule

(a) Product Pattern: The total spectrum of product, co-product and by-Product represents what is known as Product.

Plant Capacity: Factors which may affect the decision regarding plant capacity are:

(i) Market Condition
(ii) Technology
(iii) Investment cost and availability of resources
(iv) Government policies

(b) Process Selection : The first decision regarding process selection is which process to select where alternate technologies are available. For example Cement can be either by dry process or wet process. Other conditions are:

(i) Plant Capacity
(ii) Principal Inputs
(iii) Investment outlays and cost of product
(iv) Product Mix
(v) Latest development
(vi) Extent of absorption

(c) Plant Location : The choice of location depends on variety of factors:

(i) Proximity of raw materials and market

(ii) Availability of Infrastructure

(iii) Government Policies

(iv) Other factors:

- Availability of manpower, both skilled and unskilled
- Labour rate
- State of industrial relation in the place
- Climatic condition
- Recreational facilities
- General law & order condition
- Attitude of people
- Medical facilities, etc.

(d) Machineries and Equipment : The machineries and equipment required for the Project are classified into following types:

1. Plant (Process) equipment
2. Mechanical equipment
3. Electrical equipment
4. Instruments
5. Controls
6. Internal Transport system
7. Miscellaneous equipment

In each cost of the equipment, foreign exchange component is to be ascertained.

This can be an estimate. Exact price of the equipment is known when the final order is placed.

(e) Material Inputs and Utilities : Material inputs and utilities may be classified into four broad categories:

(a) Raw materials

(b) Processed industrial materials and components

(c) Auxiliary materials

(d) Utilities

(a) Raw materials : Raw materials may be any of the types:

1. Agricultural product
2. Mineral products
3. Livestock and forest product
4. Marine product

(b) Processed industrial materials and components: These may be:

1. Base Materials
2. Semi-processed materials
3. Manufactured parts, components
4. Sub-assemblies

(c) Auxiliary materials: These may be:

1. Packaging materials
2. Lubricants
3. Paints and Varnishes
4. Oil, grease
5. Miscellaneous – Other suppliers required by the factor

(d) Utilities: A broad assessment of utilities (power, water, steam,. Fuel, etc.) may be made at the time of input study through a detailed study.

Labour - Skilled, unskilled
Construction -

Financial Analysis: Following are included in the analysis:

1. Cost of project
2. Means of financing – to be elaborated separately
3. Estimates of sales and product
4. Cost of product
5. Working capital requirement
6. Profitability Projection
7. Breakeven Point
8. Projected cash flow statement
9. Projected balance sheet

Cost of Project: This is the sum of the outlays on the following:

1. Land and site development
2. Building and civil works
3. Plant and machinery
4. Technical know-how and engineering fees
5. Expenses on foreign technicians and training of Indian technicians abroad.
6. Miscellaneous fixed assets
7. Preliminary and capital issue expenses

8. Pre-operative expenses
9. Provision for contingencies
10. Margin money for working capital

Estimates of Sales and Production

1. Installed capacity
2. Number of working days
3. Number of shifts
4. Estimated product per day (Qty)
5. Estimated annual production (Qty)
6. Estimated output as percentage of plant capacity
7. Sales Qty. (after adjusting stocks)
8. Value of sales (in Rupees)

   Product:

   (i)

   (ii)

   (iii)

Cost of Production

Given the estimated production, the cost of production, the major components of cost of production are:

(i) Material cost

(ii) Utilities

(iii) Labour cost

(iv) Factory Overhead Cost

Working Capital Requirement and its Financing

1. The working capital requirement consists of the following:
   (i) Raw materials and components
   (ii) Work in Progress
   (iii) Stock of finished goods
   (iv) Debtors
   (v) Miscellaneous operating expenses

2. The principal sources of working capital finance
   (i) Working capital advances provided by the commercial banks
   (ii) Trade credit

(iii) Accruals and provision

(iv) Long term sources of finance

Profitability Projections (estimates of working result)

The estimate is prepared in the following manner:

(a) Cost of production

(b) Total administrative expenses

(c) Total sales expenses

(d) Royalty and know-how payable

(e) Total cost of production - a + b + c + d

(f) Expected sales

(g) Gross profit before interest

(h) Total financial expenses

(i) Depreciation

(j) Operating profit (g – h – i)

(k) Other income

(l) Preliminary expenses written off

(m) Profit / Loss before taxation (j + k – l)

(n) Provision for taxation

(o) Profit after tax (m – n)

Less: Dividend on - Preference capital

- Equity capital

(p) Retained profit

(q) Net cash accrual (p + l + 1)

Break-even point - (BEP): All costs are divided into fixed cost and variable cost.

Fixed cost: Fixed costs are those costs which remain unchanged for changes in volume.

Variable cost - Variable costs are those costs which vary directly with output.

Break-even point - It is the level of production at which the project neither makes profit nor incurs loss.

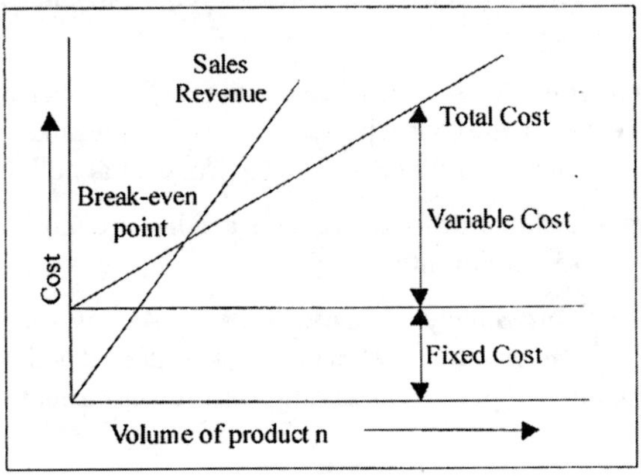

Calculation of BEP

$$\text{BEP} = \frac{\textit{Fixed Cost}}{\textit{Unit selling price} - \textit{unit variable cost}}$$

$$\text{BEP in terms of \% installed capacity} = \frac{\textit{BEP}}{\textit{Installed capacity}}$$

Project cash flow statement

Net cash flow = Profit which is retained + Depreciation + Any non-cash expenditure

Projected Balance Sheet

Based on the information on different costs, the balance sheet for the project is prepared.

Social Cost Benefit Analysis (SCBA)

SCBA or the economic analysis is project analysis for finding out social cost and benefit. In this analysis, social cost and benefit differs from the monetary cost for the following reasons:

1. Market Imperfection : The common market imperfection found in developing countries are:

(a) Rationing

(b) The prescription of minimum wage rates

(c) Foreign exchange regulation

The price by consumer under rationing is often less than the price that would have prevailed in competitive market. When minimum wages are paid, they are more than the wages paid in competitive market.

In many developing countries, official foreign exchange is made less than that in the market.

2. Externalities - A project may have both beneficial and harmful effects on society. While on one hand a project creates facilities like roads, on the other hand, it creates harmful effect like environmental pollution.

3. Taxes and Subsidies - Taxes and subsidies are monetary cost but they are considered irrelevant for social cost.

4. Concern for Savings - The concern of society for savings and investments (which leads to investment) is duly reflected in SCBA wherein a higher valuation is placed on savings and lower valuation is put on consumption.

5. Concern for Distribution - A private firm does not bother how its benefits are distributed across various groups in the society. The society, however, is concerned about the distribution of benefits across different groups. A rupee of benefit going to a poor section is considered more valuable than a rupee of benefit.

6. Merit Wants - Goals and preferences are not expressed in the market place but believed by policy makers, to be in the larger interest, may be referred to as the merit wants. For example, the government may prefer to promote an adult education or a balanced nutrition programme for school going children even though these are not sought by consumers in market place. While merit wants are not relevant from the private point of view, they are important from social point of view.

Unido Method of Project Appraisal Approach Iivolves

1. Calculation of financial profitability measured at market place
2. Obtaining net benefit of project measured in terms of economic prices
3. Adjustment for impact of the project on savings and investment
4. Adjustment for the impact of the project on income distribution
5. Adjustment for the Impact of project on merit goods whose social values differ from their economic value.

Environmental Impact Analysis

The word 'environment' is defined to include everything external to man/organism. It covers the region, surroundings or circumstances in which anything exists. This is broadly divided into two components. The first one is the aboitic or inorganic milieu, comprising the physical elements like land, water, atmosphere, climate, sound and tests. The other one is biotic or the organic milieu consisting of animals, plants, bacteria, viruses and all other living organizing.

Any development project has the following effects on nature:

1. Damage to natural resources such as air, water, land, animals and plant life.
2. Excessive pollution beyond the regenerative capacity of natural resources.
3. Accidental episodes such as release of hazardous chemicals, nuclear wastes and oil spills.

These effects are to be identified for a particular project, assessed and evaluated against the advantages accrued.

Special attention should be given on the impact on:

(1) Air pollution

(2) Water pollution

(3) Human habitat

(4) Solid waste

3

Project Finance

2. Project Finance

It is a method of financing very large capital intensive projects with long gestation period where the lenders rely on the assets created for the project as security and the cash flow generated by the project as source of funds for repaying their dues. Project finance is the financing of long term infrastructure and industrial projects based upon the complex financial structure where project debt and equity are used to finance the project, and debt is repaid using the cash flow generated by operation of the project, rather than the general assets or creditworthiness of he project sponsors. Because of this structure, the debt is said to be 'non-recourse' to the project sponsors.

The financing is typically secured by all of the project assets, including the revenue-producing contracts. Project lenders are given a lien on all of these assets, and are able to assume control of a project if the project company has difficulties complying with the loan terms.

Generally, a special purpose entity is created for each project, thereby shielding other assets owned by a project sponsor from the detrimental effect of a project failure. As a special purpose entity, the project company has no assets other than the project. Capital contribution commitments by the owners of the project are sometimes necessary to ensure that the project is financially sound.

Project finance is often more complicated and more expensive than alternative financing methods. It is most commonly utilized in the mining, transportation, telecommunication and public utility industries which are subject to a number of insurmountable technical, environmental, economic and political risks. To cope with these risks, projects in these industries (such as power plants or railway lines) are generally completed by a number of specialist companies operating in a contractual network with each other. The various patterns of implementation are known as 'project delivery methods'.

The financing of these projects often distributed among multiple parties, so as to distribute the risk associated with the project while simultaneously ensuring profits for each part involved. Usually, a project scheme involves a number of equity inventors, known as sponsors, as well as a syndicate of banks which provide loans to the operation. The loans are most commonly non-recourse loans which are secured by the project itself and paid entirely from its cash flow. A riskier or more expansive project may require limited recourse financing secured by a surety from sponsors. A complex project finance scheme may incorporate corporate finance, securitization, options, insurance provisions or other further measures to mitigate risk.

Means of Finance

- Share capital
- Term loan
- Debenture capital
- Deferred credit
- Incentive sources
- Miscellaneous sources

Share Capital: There are two types of share capital – equity capital and preference capital. Equity capital represents the contribution made by the owners of the business, the equity shareholders, who enjoy the rewards and bear the risks of ownership. Equity capital being risk capital carries no fixed rate of dividend. Preference capital represents the contribution made by preference shareholders and the dividend paid on it is generally fixed.

Term Loans: Provided by financial institutions and commercial banks, term loans represent secured borrowings which are very important sources (and often the major source) for financing new project as well as expansion, modernization and renovation scheme of existing firms. There are two broad types of term loans available in India's rupee term loan and foreign currency term loans. While former are given for financing land, building, civil works, indigenous plant and machinery and so on, the later are provided for meeting the foreign currency expenditure towards impart of equipments and technical know-how.

Debenture Capital: Akin of promissory notes, debentures are instruments for raising debt capital. Debt is that which is owed; referencing assets owned, but the term can cover other obligations. In the case of assets, debt is a means of using future purchasing power in the present before a summation has been earned. Some companies and corporations use debt as a part of their overall corporate finance strategy. A debt is created when a creditor agree to lend a sum of assets to a debtor. In modern society, debt is usually granted with expected repayment; in many cases, plus interest. Historically, debt was responsible for the creation of indentured servants. The debenture can be of two types NCD (non-convertible debenture) and CD (convertible debenture). The different between the two is former could not be converted into equity capital but latter could be converted into the equity share capital of the company.

Deferred Credit: Many a time the suppliers of plant and machinery offer a deferred credit facility under which payment for the purchase of plant and machinery can be made over a period of time.

Incentive Sources: The government and its agency may provide the financial support as incentive to certain types of promoters or for setting up industrial units in certain locations. These incentives may take the form of send capital assistance. (Provided at the nominal rate of interest to enable the promoter to meet his contribution to the projects), or capital subsidy (to attract industries to certain locations), or tax deferment or exemption (particularly from sales tax, excise duty and other levies by the local government). The recent measure taken by the government in developing the SEZ.

Miscellaneous Sources: A small portion of project finance may come from miscellaneous sources like unsecured loans, public deposits and leasing and hire purchase finance. Unsecured loans are typically provided by the promoters to bridge the gap between the promoters contribution (as required by the financial institutions) and the equity capital the promoters can subscribe to Public deposit represent unsecured borrowing from the public at large. Leasing and hire purchase finance represent a form of borrowing from the conventional term loans and debenture capital.

4

Project Appraisal

4. Project Appraisal

The principal issue considered and the criteria employed in such appraisals.

4.1. Market Appraisal

1. Examine the reasonableness of the demand projections by utilizing the findings of the available surveys industry association projection, planning commission /DOTD. Projections and independent market surveys (which may sometimes by commissioned).
2. Assess the adequacy of the marketing infrastructure in the terms of promotional effort, distribution network, transport facilities, stock levels, etc.
3. Judge the knowledge, experience and competence of key marketing personnel.

4.2 Technical Appraisal

Financial institutions focus mainly on the following aspects:

1. Product mix
2. Capacity
3. Process of manufacture
4. Engineering know-how and technical collaboration
5. Raw material and consumption
6. Location and site
7. Building

8. Plant and equipment
9. Manpower requirement
10. Break-even Point

4.3 Financial Appraisal

4.3.1 Reasonableness of Estimate of Capital Cost

While assessing the capital cost estimate, efforts are made to ensure:

1. Padding or under estimation of cost avoided
2. Specification of machinery is proper
3. Proper quotations are obtained from potential suppliers
4. Contingencies are provided
5. Inflation factors are provided

4.3.2 Reasonableness of the Estimate of Working Results

The estimate of working result is sought to be based on:

(a) A realistic market demand forecast
(b) Price computations for inputs and outputs that are based on current quotations and inflationary factors.
(c) An appropriate time schedule for capacity utilization
(d) Cost projections that distinguish between fixed and variable costs.

4.3.3 Financial Appraisal Method

Introduction - A project should earn sufficient return on investment. As such, an analysis has to be made on the project. Such analysis broadly falls under two categories:

1. Non-discounted cash flow techniques which include:
   (i) Payback period method
   (ii) Accounting rate of return (ARR)
2. Discounted cash flow techniques which include:
   (i) Net present value (NVP) method
   (ii) Profitability Index (PI) method
   (iii) Internal Rate of Return (IRR) method

4.3.2.1 Payback Period Method

Pay back is defined as the length of time required to recover the original investment in the project.

Ex. Initial Investment - Rs.1, 00,000/-

Cash flow:

1st year	-	Rs. 10,000/-
2nd year	Rs. 15,000/-	
3rd year	Rs. 20,000/-	
4th year	-	Rs. 25,000/-
5th year	-	Rs. 30,000/-
6th year	-	Rs. 35,000/-

$$\text{Payback period} = \frac{1{,}00{,}000}{10{,}000 + 15{,}000 + 20{,}000 + 25{,}000 + 30{,}000} = 5\ years$$

Accounting Rate of Return (ARR)

The average rate of return is also called Accounting rate of return.

$$\text{ARR} = \frac{\text{Profit after tax}}{\text{Book Value of the Investment}}$$

Ex. Average profit over the life of the project = Rs. 4,50,000
Average investment during the life = Rs. 12,00,000

$$\text{ARR} = \frac{4{,}50{,}000}{12{,}00{,}000} = 37.5\%$$

Net Present Value (NPV) method

NPV = Sum of present value – Initial investment of future cash in flows

Symbolically:

$$\text{NPV} = \frac{CF_1}{(1+r)^1} + \frac{CF_2}{(1+r)^2} + \frac{CF_3}{(1+r)^3} + \cdots \frac{CF_n}{(1+r)^n}] - \text{Initial investment}$$

Or more generally

$$\text{NPV} = \frac{\text{Sum of present value of}}{\text{future cash in flows}} - \frac{\text{Sum of present value of}}{\text{cash outflows}}$$

Where, CF_1, CF_2, CF_3, ...CF_n future cash in flows from 1st year n year

n = life of project in year
r = discount rate or cost of capital
CF_0 = present value of cash outflows

If NPV =0 the project may be taken or rejected
NPV < 1 Reject the project
NPV > 1 Accept the project

Ex. Find out the NPV for a project from the following information

Investment for the project - Rs. 10, 00,000
Life of the project - 5 years
Cost of capital - 13%

Year	1	2	3	4	5
Cash in flow (in Rs.)	3,00,000	4,00,000	4,00,000	3,00,000	2,00,000

Sol^n. : Present value of cash in flow

$$= \frac{CF_1}{(1+r)^1} + \frac{CF_2}{(1+r)^2} + \frac{CF_3}{(1+r)^3} + \frac{CF_4}{(1+r)^4} + \frac{CF_5}{(1+r)^5}$$

$$= \frac{3,00,000}{(1+0.13)^1} + \frac{4,00,000}{(1+0.13)^2} + \frac{4,00,000}{(1+0.13)^3} + \frac{3,00,000}{(1+0.13)^4} + \frac{2,00,000}{(1+0.13)^5}$$

= 2,65,487 + 3,13,259 + 2,77,219 + 1,83,993 + 1,08,548 = Rs. 11,48,506

NPV = 11,48,506 – 10,00,000 = 1,48,506

Since NPV > 1, the project may be accepted.

4.3.3.2 <u>Profitability Index</u>

$$\text{Profitability Index (PI)} = \frac{\text{Present value of cash inflow}}{\text{Initial Investment}}$$

When comparing between projects, project having higher PI is selected.

From our earlier example:

$$PI = \frac{11,48,506}{10,00,000} = 10148$$

In general accept project with PI>1.

4.3.3.4 Internal Rate of Return (IRR)

It is that discount rate that makes NPV equal to zero.

NPV =0

or, it is that discount rate where

$$\text{Sum of Present Value of future cash inflows} = \text{Initial Cash inflow}$$

Ex. Calculate the IRR on the basis of Project data given.

Year	Cash outflow	Cash inflow
0	Rs. 1000000	——
1		Rs. 400000
2		Rs. 250000
3		Rs. 250000
4		Rs. 200000
5		Rs. 200000
6		Rs. 100000

Sol^n : Let us assume r = 12% p.a.

Present value of cash inflows

$$=\frac{400000}{(1+0.12)^1}+\frac{250000}{(1+0.12)^2}+\frac{200000}{(1+0.12)^3}+\frac{200000}{(1+0.12)^4}+\frac{200000}{(1+0.12)^5}+\frac{100000}{(1+0.12)^6}$$

= Rs. 1050979

Since it is > 1000000

We assume r = 14%

In the similar fashion we calculate the sum of present value which is

= Rs. 1002586 which is slightly less than Rs. 1000000.

So actual value of 'r' which makes sum of present value of future cash inflows equal to initial investment lies between 14% and 15%. By interpolating, we get –

$$\text{IRR} = 14\% + \frac{(15-14)(1002586-1000000)}{(1002586-979879)} \text{ x } 100$$

= 14% + 0.1139% = 14.1139% =14.114%

4.3.3.5 Key Financial Indicators

1. Internal Rate of Return
2. Debt Service Cover Rate

$$=\frac{\text{Profit after Tax} + \text{Depreciation} + \text{Other non} - \text{cash charge} + \text{Interest of long Term Loan}}{\text{Interest on Term Loan} + \text{Repayment of Term Loan}}$$

3. Break Even Point (BEP)
4. BEP in terms of Installed Capacity
5. Profit Margin on Sales

$$= \frac{\text{Profit after Tax}}{\text{Sales}}$$

6. Debt Equity Ratio $= \frac{\text{Long Term Debt}}{\text{Equity}}$

7. Current Ratio $= \frac{\text{Current Asset}}{\text{Current Liability}}$

8. ROI (after tax) $= \frac{\text{Profit after Tax} + \text{Depreciation} + \text{Interest on Loan (1} - \text{tax rate}}{\text{Cost of Project}}$

4.3.4 Economic Appraisal

The economic review looks at the project from the larger social point of view. The methodology adopted by the financial institutions for the purpose of (also referred to as Social Cost Benefit Analysis) is labeled as 'Partial Little Mirrless' approach they also look at two other economic indicators :

(i) Effective rate of protection

(ii) Domestic resource cost

4.3.5 Managerial Appraisal

In order to judge the managerial capability of the promoters the following questions are raised:

(a) How resourceful are the promoters?

(b) How sound is the understanding of the project by the promoters?

(c) How committed are the promoters?

Resourcefulness: This judge in terms of the prior experience of the promoters, the progress achieved in organizing various aspects of the project and the skill with which the project is presented.

Understanding: This is assessed in terms of the credibility of the project plan including inter alia, the organization structure, the estimated cost, the financing pattern the assessment of various inputs and the marketing programme and the details furnished to the financial institution.

Commitment: This is gauged by the resources (financial, managerial and other) applied short term as well as the long term are pursued. Managerial review also involves as assessment of the caliber of the key technical and managerial personnel working on the project the schedule for training thou and the remuneration structure for rewarding and motivating them.

5

Project Organisation and Contract Management

5. Project Organisation and Contracts Management

Once a project has been established and goal are set it is necessary to organize the work in such a manner that implementation is effective. Traditional organization is not suitable for the purpose.

5.1 Project Manager as a staff assistant to the Chief Executive

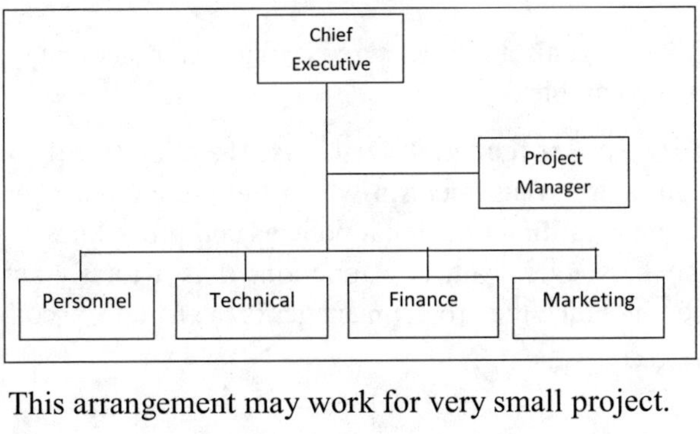

This arrangement may work for very small project.

5.2 Consultant as a Project Manager

This is similar to earlier organization. But problem starts with where line managers do not respond to the Project Manager authority. He does not have authority over the line managers.

5.3 Matrix Organisation

In this arrangement the sharing of authority between a project manager and other functional managers in formalized.

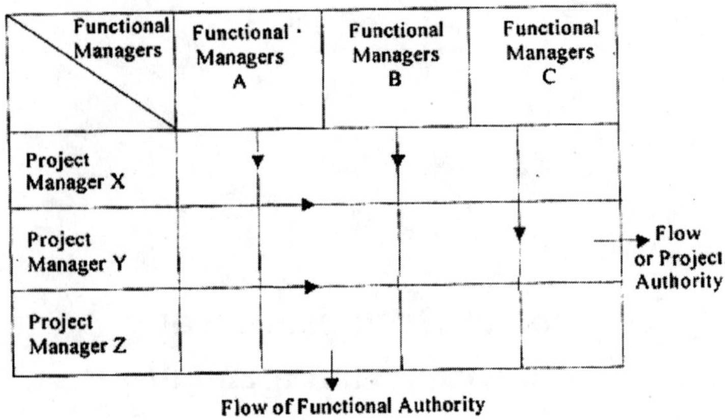

1. Dual reporting is a problem
2. Each project has to follow the rules of the parent department
3. Some time functional manager overloads the staff assigned to the project

5.4 Taskforce Organisation: While in Matrix Organization team members report to both Project Authority and functional authority creating problem a Task Force Organisation team members report only to Project authority.

Both these organization structure is suitable for medium type project with not much complexity.

5.5 Totally Project zed Organisation: A totally projected organization is an arrangement in which the project manager has total authority even regarding functional policies and procedures. There is no constraint whatsoever w.r.t. any function. It is a totally autonomous organization in which the project manager is the Chief Executive.

Chief Executive

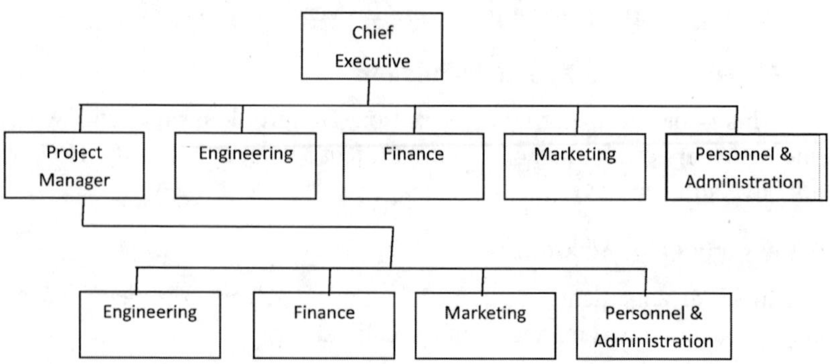

5.6 Turnkey Contract: In a turnkey contract a single contractor has complete responsibility to supply owner a plant which is complete and ready for the owner to operate by simply turning or the key.

5.7 Work Breakdown Structure and Work Package: Systematic distribution of work starts with breaking down the whole project systematically into successive levels by using what is known as WBS (Work Breakdown Structure).

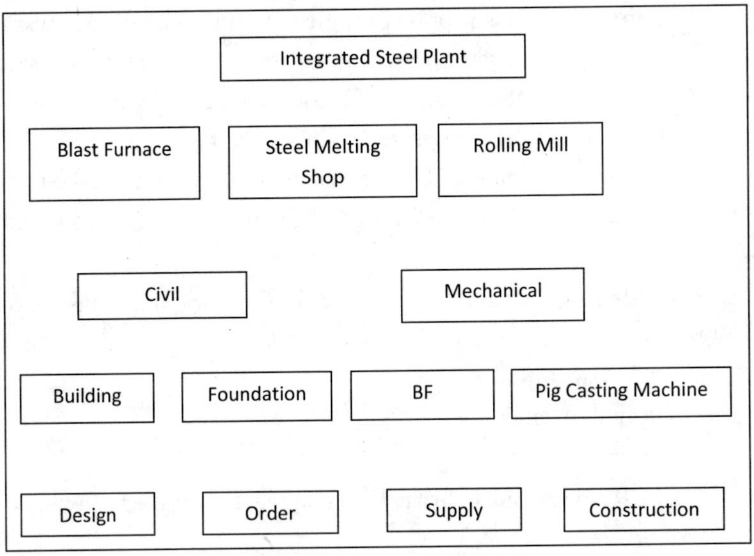

5.8 Work Package : Can be viewed as the smallest division of work where it still retains the multidisciplinary Characteristics of a project. The first step is in preparing the WBS. Individually or several packages combined together may form a contract features of W.P.

1. Time and cost targets can be attached each WP which are numbered.
2. Used for cost collection and cost control.

5.9 Contracts : The organization arrangement accords the project manager appropriate authority over the in house resources. But not all projects can be executed within house resources and the project manager has to requisition extra organization resources for the execution of the project. When a project manager has to get things done with resources over which he has no direct authority, it become necessary to acquire the required authority in lieu of some consideration. Such an arrangement can be termed as a contract and the authority so acquired as contractual authority.

Business Contract : A contract as such is an agreement between two or more parties in writing to do or not to do certain things. Business contracts are those agreements, which are enforceable at law under the Indian Contract Act 1872. The sequence of events in a business contract.

Enquiry	Issue of NIT (Notice Inviting Tender) to newspapers By the project authority and sale of tender document
Offer	Submission of tender document by the bidder
Acceptance	By the project authority of the offer
Agreement	Signed by competent authority of both the parties
Contract	The agreement is given a legal form on stamped paper

5.10 3R of Contracts: The three R of contracting consists of the following:

- Responsibility
- Reimbursement
- Risk

5.10.1 Responsibility: In a typical contract covers the following issues such as:

(a) What to parcel out to contractor and what to retain.

(b) How to define the work parcels so that the contractors know their scope precisely and there is no overlapping undefined, unallocated or ambiguous work areas.

(c) What are relevant performance parameters for fulfillment of which contractors must assume responsibility.

5.10.2 Owner doing everything except manufacture of plant and machinery

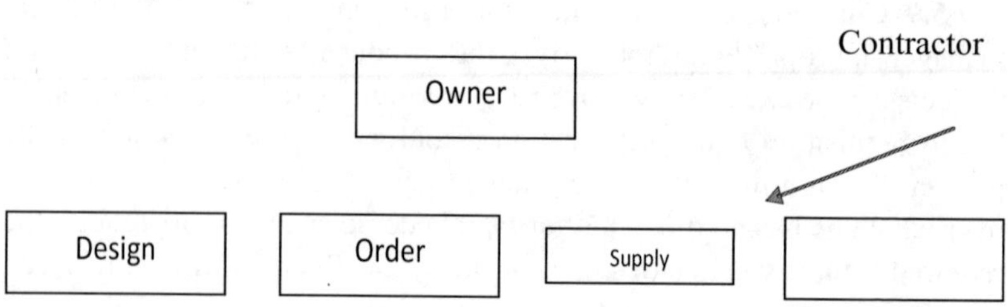

5.10.3 Owner assuming the task of ordering and carrying out project management through contracts

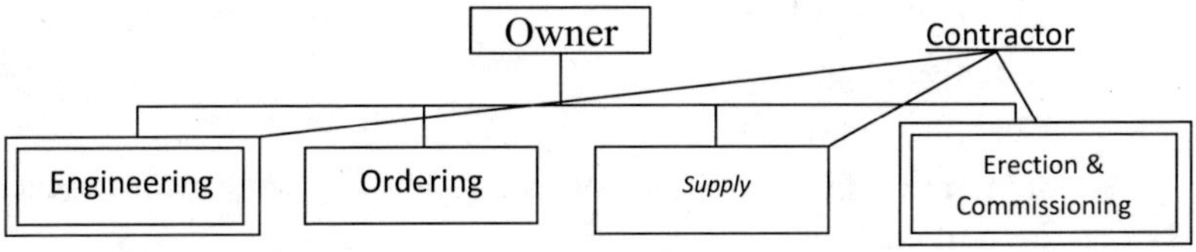

5.10.4 Owner engages a consultant for engineering and project management services

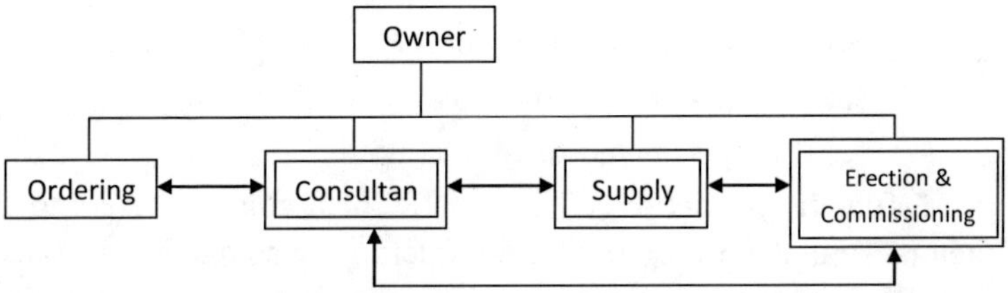

5.10.5 Owner engages no. of agencies for specified work packages. But integrating service is kept with owner or something consultant is appointed

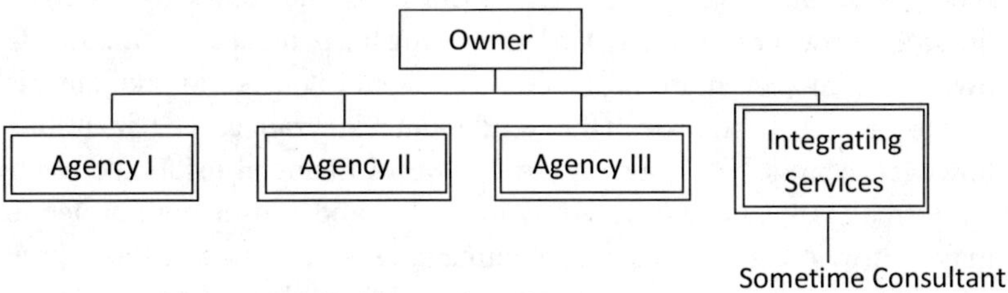

5.10.6 Owner hands over the entire responsibility of project execution to a prime contractor

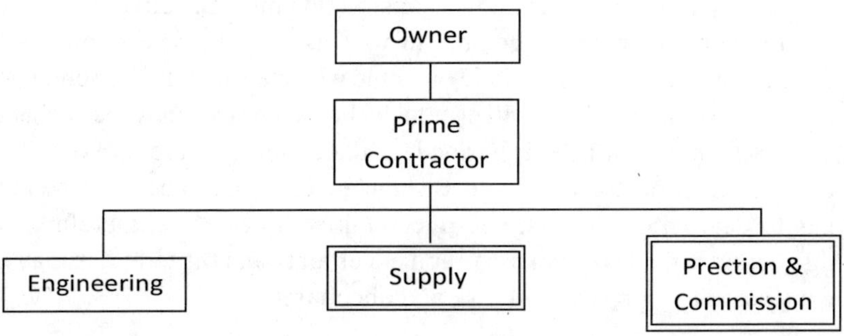

5.10.7 Reimbursement: Arrangement for reimbursement a contractor for the services rendered by him.

Types of reimbursement

1. Lump sum contracts
2. Cost plus contracts
3. Item rate contracts – based on rates quoted by contractor for each item of contract
4. Convertible contracts – starts with cost plus when scope of work is not defined later convert it to lump sum
5. Hybrid contract
   (a) Lump sum and item rate
   (b) Lump sum and cost plus
   (c) Lump sum and fixed rate

5.10.8 Risk Factor : The last 'R' of a contract refers to the risk factors. Both the owner and the contractors are so much concerned about this 'R' that most of the pages of a contract deal with only this matter. In fact, a contract is considered to be an instrument for transfer of risk from the owner to the contractor and necessarily this should evoke some resistance from the contractor. The least that a contractor would do is to seek protection in one from or other. But while the contractor risks only his fee, the owner runs the risk of not having his plant at all. Naturally, the owner would seek more protection and would not like to take any risk against which he does not have adequate insurance. The insurance, however, cannot be always in the form of a financial insurance policy. Only small risk can be covered by insurance and a little more protection may be provided in the contract document. However, most of the risks are usually covered when contracts are awarded through a proven contracting process.

Risk and Uncertainty : Theoretically risk are associated with which probability can be associated. In a construction project, neither the owner nor the contractor would be able to forecast the outcome in all cases. Them is only a vague anxiety the outcome which each of there apprehends may not be best. But that it will eventually be, no one can know beforehand. Such a situation is usually termed as uncertain. A there are very few outcome in a construction project which are certain, project management has to deal with only risk and uncertainties. In practice, therefore, no distinction is made between risk and uncertainty and the term risk may be considered to represent both risk and uncertainly.

Identification of risk : Let us identify the risk which either the owner or the contractor may face. What the owner is not certain about and, therefore, considers as a risk may be any of the following:

1. Will the contractor be able to carry out the work as per specification?
2. Can the work be completed within the quoted cost?
3. Will the plant perform at the required level?
4. Will the contractor stay on the job till its completion?
5. Will the contractor adhere to the time schedule?
6. Will the contractor meet the owner's requirement if they are changed at a late date?
7. Will the contractor co-operate with the owner and third parties?
8. Will the party submitting the tender back out when the contract is awarded to him?
9. Will the contractor leave behind liability for the owners do deal with in regard to his staff or third parties?
10. Will the contractor rectify defects discovered after he leaves the scene?
11. Does the contractor understand his intent fully and interpret the contractual terms as the owner would?
12. If the relationship does not click, what can happen?

The contractor, similarly, is also not certain about many things. In particular, he carries the following risks in relation to the owner would seek protection against the same in the contract.

1. Will the owner terminate his work before completion of the same?
2. Will the owner make payments promptly?
3. Will there be work hold-up and imposed idleness for him?
4. Will the owner carry certain minimum obligations regarding his work?
5. Will the owner change the scope of work upsetting his plan and estimates?
6. Will the work quantities and specifications charge significantly affecting his rates?
7. Will he get reimbursed for extended work duration?
8. Will there be price escalation and will he get compensated for the same?

9. Will he be penalized for failures beyond his control?
10. Will there be smooth cash flow?
11. Will the owner provide workforce and other inputs in time for uninterrupted progress?
12. Will the plant or equipment be taken over when ready?
13. Will the owner honour extra claims?
14. Will there be difference in interpretation of his scope and responsibilities with the owner?
15. Can he make a profit?

General Conditions of Contract (GCC): To ensure that parties entering into a contract are appropriately protected against risks, various professional institutions, have devised standard contract documents. It is advisable for the parties concerned to take-up onw of these documents for framing their contract rather than making one of their own. When published conditions of contract are used, they are likely to be more neutral than those made in house which may be slanted either towards the owner of the contractor depending on who drafts the samr. Use of published conditions of contract will also avoid unnecessary discussions which normally follow when in house drafted condition of contraction are used.

The Institution of Mechanical Engineering (IME), UK has developed such forms for various types of work which have international acceptance. These forms, in fact, have been developed jointly by three institutions:

1. The institution of Mechanical Engineers (IME)
2. The Institution of Electrical Engineers (IEE)
3. Association of Consulting Engineers (ACE)

In India the National Association of consulting Engineers (NACE) has also developed standard forms which could be used for this purpose.

A model form usually contains various clauses, which specify the exact position in respect of various risk factors.

6

Project Implementation

6.1 Network Planning

6.2 Project Direction and Coordination

6.3 Project Control

6.1 Network Planning - PERT/CPM

Structure

6.1 Introduction

6.1.2 Network Analysis

6.1.2.1 Objectives

6.1.2.2 Application of Network

6.1.2.3 Key elements in Network

6.1.2.4 Constructing the Network

6.1.3 Time Estimates in Network

6.1.4 Critical Path Method (CPM)

Programme Evaluation and Review Technique (PERT)

6.1.1 Introduction: A project is successful when it is completed on time, within the budgeted cost and to technical specification which satisfies the end users. In this respect, the Network techniques are the most powerful tool for planning scheduling and controlling CPM/PERT are the two most important Network Techniques.

Prior to PERT/CPM, the most popular techniques for project scheduling was the bar chart or Gantt chart developed by Henry I. Gantt around 1900. The main limitation of this technique is its inability to show the interrelationship and inter dependency among many activities which are involved in a project. To overcome such limitations, these two techniques PERT/CPM were developed. While PERT was developed by U.S. Navy for their Polaris Missile programme, CPM was developed by Du Point company for their projects independently around 1959. The whole purpose was to reduce the completion time for the project.

6.1.2 Network Analysis : Network is basically a graphic representation of all the activities in a project showing the inter-relationship and inter dependencies between the activities. This also shows those activities which are critical for the project completion so that Management can concentrate on those activities.

6.1.2.1 Objective

(a) Powerful tool for planning, scheduling and control

(b) Minimization of Time and Cost

(C) Minimization of idle resources

6.1.2.2 Application of Network:

(a) Construction of River Dams, Bridges, Roadways, Stadium, Metro Rail

(b) Maintenance and over hauling of complex machineries

(c) Implementation of modern management system like computerization

(d) Staff Development programme

(e) Product launching

(f) R&D Project

(g) Even Management, etc.

6.1.2.3 Key elements in Network:

Activity: All projects may be viewed as being composed of operations or tasks called activities. An activity is represented by an arrow. The head of the arrow shows the flow of activities. An activity consumes time and resources.

Event : An activity represent a specific accomplishment in the project and does not consume time or resources. It is represented by a circle O.

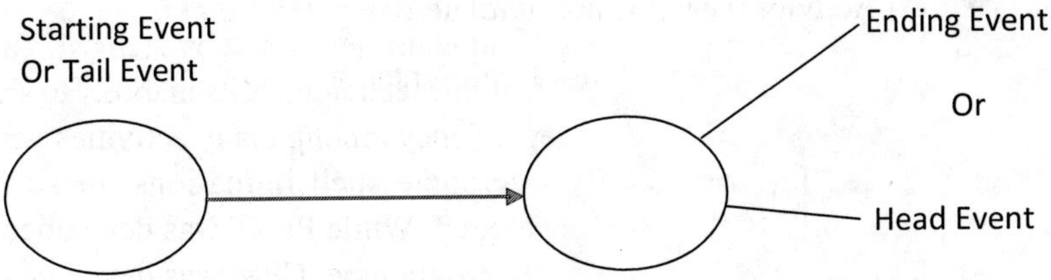

Ex: Foundation completed – Ending event
Design Started – Starting event

Dummy Activity – An activity, which does not consume time or resources and represented by (   )

This used to

(i) Make activities with common starting and finishing events distinguishable
(ii) To maintain the precedence relationship

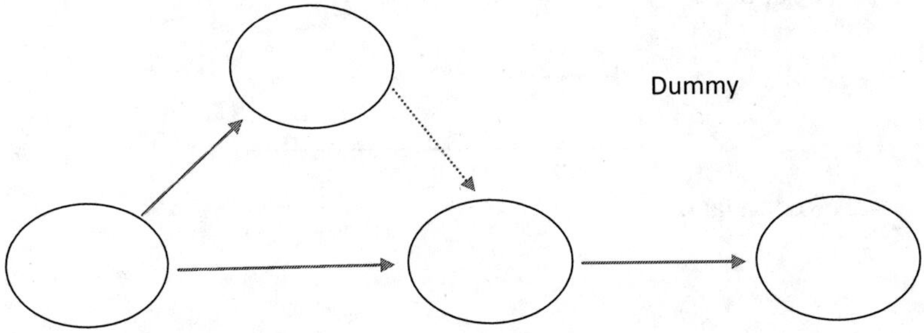

Interdependence:

A project is made up of many activities, which are interrelated. The first step is to break up the whole project into a number of smaller activities and find out their interdependence relationship following question are asked:

(a) Which other activities must be completed before this activity can start (Precedence)
(b) What other activities can be done while this activity is being done (Concurrence)

(c) What activity or activities cannot start until after this activity is done? (Subsequence)

Ex.: (a) Activity B cannot start until activities A is complete

Network Representation

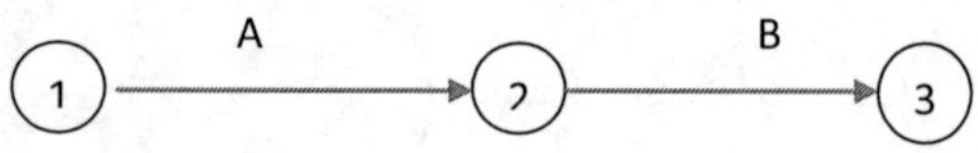

(b) B and C start after A

(c) A and B are concurrent C start after A & B

Common Errors in Network Drawing:

(a) Dangling

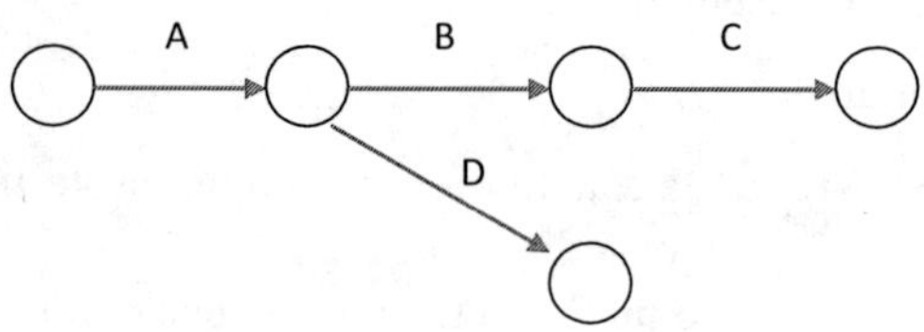

(b) Looping

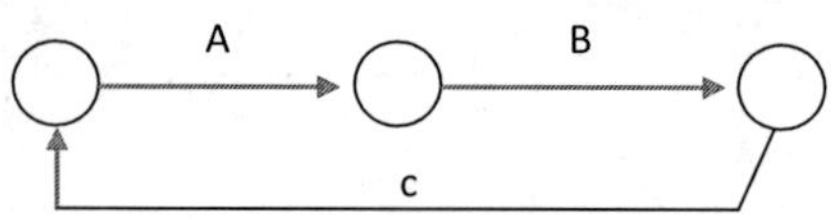

(c) Redundancy

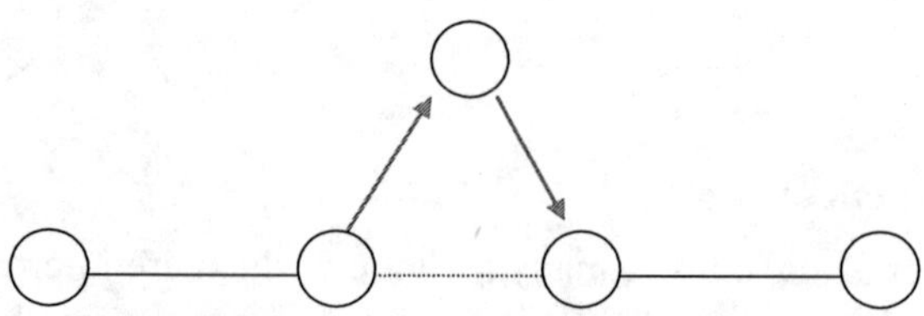

Event Numbering

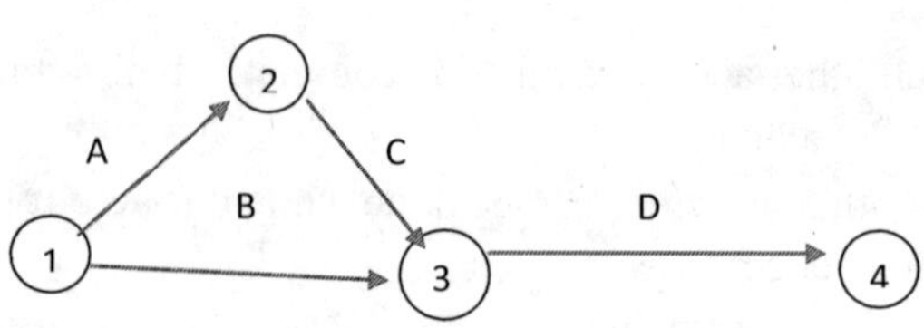

Rule:

1. Head Event No. should be more than the tail Event no.
2. Activity is denoted by the event no.

   Activity A – denoted by 1 – 2

   Activity B – denoted by 1 – 3

   Activity C – denoted by 2 – 3

   Activity D – denoted by 3 – 4

Worked out Examples:

1. Prepare a network diagram based on the following sequences number the events.

Activity	Predecessor Activity
A	---
B	---
C	A
D	B,C

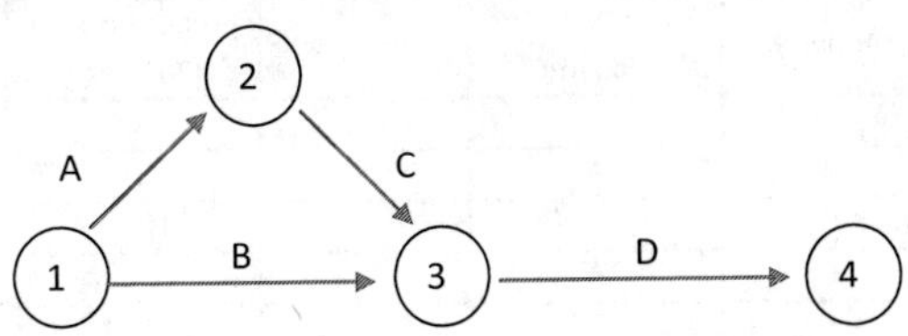

2. Prepare a network diagram based on the following sequences and number the events.

Activity	Predecessor Activity
A	---
B,C,D	A
E	B
F	D

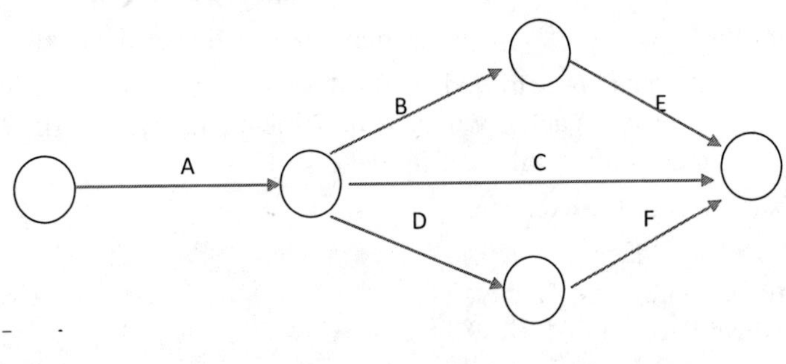

Exercise

1. Prepare the network with following sequences and number the events.

Activity	Predecessor Activity
A	---
B,C,	A
D	B
E	C, D

2. Prepare the network with following sequences and number the events.

Activity	Predecessor Activity
A, B, C	---
D	A, B
E	C
F	E
G	A
H	G, D, F

1. Draw network diagram for the following activities:

Activity	Predecessor or Activity	Activity	Predecessor or Activity
A	---	G	C
B	A	H	C, D
C	A	I	E, F
D	A	---	---
E	B	J	G, H
F	C	K	I, J

6.1.3 Time estimate in Network Analysis

Key elements

TE = Earliest start time of an event

TL – Latest start time of an event

Time Estimate: In CPM only one time estimate for each activity is taken.

Critical Path: The longest path in a network is called critical path.

Let us take a example to find out the duration of the project taking one time estimate for each activity. This is in Critical Path Method (CPM). In PERT the time estimate will be different.

Example 3 of the exercise.

Duration in days
Project Duration – 42 days
Critical Path – 1-2-4-7-8-9

Forward Pass: Calculate the TE for all events. For any event highest time taking path will be taken and that is the TE or earliest start time of an event.

Backward Pass: Calculate the TL of all events starting with the end event of the project. For any event lowest time taking path will be taken and that is the TL or latest start of an event.

Critical Path: Mark the path, which is longest time taking path. Please note that for events and the critical paths TE and TL are the same. Critical path may be denoted by double line with hatch.

Project Duration: The total time taken by the critical path is project duration.

Calculation of Early Start (ES), Early Finish (EF), Late Start (LS), Late Finish (LF), Total Float (TF), Free Float (FF) and Independent Float (IF) of an activity.

Early Start – ES of an activity is the earliest time an activity can start

Early Finish – EF of an activity is the earliest time an activity can finish

Late Start - LS of an activity is the latest time an activity can start.

Late Finish – LF of an activity is the latest time an activity can finish

Total Float – The amount of time by which completion of an activity could be delayed beyond the earliest completion time without affecting the overall project duration time.

TF = (TL of Head Event) – (TE of the tail Event + Duration of the activity)

Free Float – The amount of time by which completion of an activity can be delayed beyond the earliest finish time without affecting the earliest start of a subsequent activity.

FF = TE of Head Event – (TL of the Tail Event + Duration of the activity)

Independent Float – The amount of time by which start of an activity can be delayed without affecting the earliest start time of any immediately following activities assuming that the preceding activity has finished at the latest finish time.

Independent Float (IF) = TE of Head Event –(TL of Tail Event + Duration of Activity)

Example 1: The following table given the activities in a construction project.

Activity	1-2	1-3	2-3	2-4	3-4	4-5
Duration in days	20	25	10	12	6	10

(i) Draw the network diagram of the project

(ii) Find the critical path and project duration

(iii) Calculate ES, EF, LS, LF, Total Float (TF), Free Float (FF) & Independent Float (IF) for each activity.

(i) Network Diagram

(ii) Critical Path 1 - 2 - 3 - 4 - 5

Project duration – 46 days

(iii) ES, EF, LS, LF, TF, FF AND IF

Programme Evaluation and Review Technique (PERT)

The critical path method (CPM) use only one time estimate for each activity. But PERT uses three time estimates to overcome the uncertainly in project time estimates.

(i) Most optimistic time - a
(ii) Most pessimistic time - b
(iii) Most likely time - m

Most optimistic time: It is shortest possible time in which an activity can be completed in an ideal condition.

Most pessimistic time: It is maximum possible time in which an activity can be completed under worst condition.

Most likely time: It is the time in which an activity can be completed under moral condition.

Expected time: $te = \frac{a + 4m + b}{6}$

The formula is a linear approximation of beta distribution whose accuracy is considered reasonably sufficient.

After having arrived the Expected time (te) for each activity the critical path is found out by making forward pass and backward pass computations, calculating Earliest Start Time (TE) and Latest Start Time (TI) of all events.

Example:

Draw PERT network diagram from the following data. Arrive at critical path and estimated project duration.

Activity	Preceeding Activity	Optimistic Time (week)	Most Likely Time	Pessimistic Time(week)
A	--	2	5	8
B	--	4	6	8
C	A	3	5	7
D	B	1	3	5
E	C, D	2	5	8
F	C, D	3	4	7
G	E	4	5	12
H	I	1	4	9
I	F, H	5	6	13

Probability Aspects of Project Completion Time

If the activity timings are definite, in all likely load the period completion will also be definite. The probability of completing the project within the estimated project time arises in PERT calculation because the activity time estimates are not definite but uncertain PERT takes into account uncertainties in activity time and hence arrives at three different time estimates. This result in activity time having variances and hence the total

Activity	Optimistic Time	Pessimistic Time	Most likely time	Expected Time $te = \frac{a + 4m + b}{6}$
A	2	8	5	5
B	4	8	6	6
C	3	7	5	5
D	1	5	3	3
E	2	8	5	5
F	3	7	4	5
G	4	12	5	6
H	1	9	4	5
I	5	13	6	7

project time will also have variances. It is assumed the expected completion time (te) follows normal distribution with variance equal to sum of variances of all activities on critical path.

$$\text{Variance of an Activity} = \sigma^2 = (\frac{b - a^2}{6})$$

$$\text{Standard Dev.} \quad = \sigma = \frac{b - a}{6}$$

Prob.: A small project consisting eight activities has the following characteristics.

Activity	Preceeding Activity	Most Optimistic Time (a)	Most Likely (m)	Most Pessimistic (b)
A	--	2	4	12
B	--	10	12	26
C	A	8	9	10
D	A	10	15	20
E	A	7	7.5	11
F	B, C	9	9	9
G	D	3	3.5	7
H	E, F, G	5	5	5

(i) Draw the PERT network for the project

(ii) Determine the critical path

(iii) Prepare the activity schedule for the project

(iv) If a 30 weeks deadline is imported, what is the probability that the project will be finished within the time limit?

(v) If the project Manager wants to be 99% sure that the project is completed in time how many weeks before that time should be start the project work?

Solution :

The expected time and variance of each activity is worked out by using the formula:

$$\text{te} = \frac{a + 4m + b}{6} \text{and variance} = \sigma^n = (\frac{b - a^2}{6})$$

By using the expected activity time (the) the PERT network is drawn as under.

Calculation for activity duration times and scheduling times.

Activity	a	m	b	te	$\sigma 2$	Early		Late	
						Start	Finish	Start	Finish
A	2	4	12	5	25/9	0	5	0	5
B	10	12	25	14	64/9	0	14	1	15
C	8	9	10	9	1/9	5	14	6	15
D	10	15	20	15	25/9	5	20	5	20
E	7	7.5	11	8	4/9	5	13	16	24
F	9	9	9	9	0	14	23	15	24
G	3	3.5	7	4	4/9	20	24	20	24
H	5	5	5	5	0	24	29	24	29

The critical path of the project is 1-3-4-5-6 the critical activities being A-D-G-H

Expected time of completion of the project = 5+15+4+5=29 week

Project variance is calculated by adding variances of critical activities

$$= \frac{25}{9} + \frac{25}{9} + 0 = 6$$

The required probability can be determined by finding the area under normal curve to the left of X = 30.

Now, probability of completing the project within 30 week deadline is:

$P\ (x \leq 30) = 0.5 + p(\mu < X < 30) = 0.5 + P(0 \leq Z \leq 0.41))\text{where } Z = \frac{X-\mu}{\sqrt{\sigma 2}} = \frac{30-29}{\sqrt{6}}$

$= 0.5 + 0.1591 = 0.6591$

Or 65.91 % probability

If the project shirt X weeks before due date, X ill represent the ordinate under normal curve to the left of which 99% area lies.

The area between and X being (99-50) or 49% and 'z' value corresponding to this is 2.33 (from tables)

$$2.33 = \frac{X - 29}{\sqrt{6}} \text{ or } X = 29 + 2.33\sqrt{6} = 34.7 \text{ weeks}$$

PERT Cost or Crashing of Project Network

The execution of project involves two types of costs.

Indirect Cost: Consists of overheads, office expenditure, administrative costs, penalty for delay etc. The indirect cost varies with time. Any reduction in project duration reduces the indirect cost.

Direct Cost: Includes cost of material, machinery used in project and payments made by labours and sub-contractors if any. At the time of estimating the duration of an activity it was assumed normal amount of labour and machineries will be used. When it is considered to reduce the activity time more resources are required to be employed so the cost will increase when the time is reduced. But a time will reach when the time cannot be futher reduced with additional resources. This relationship is shown in the following figure.

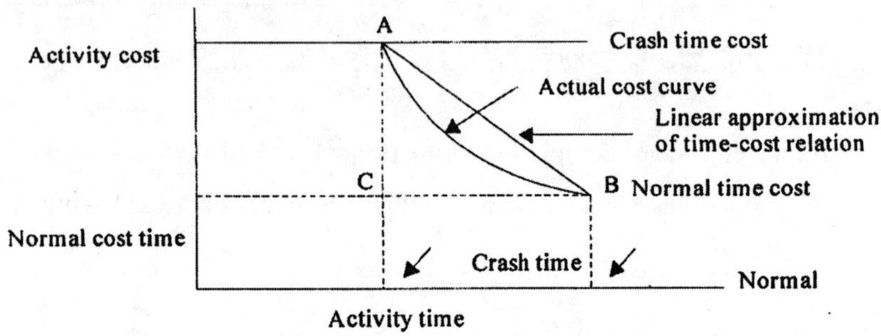

Time – Cost Relationship

$$\text{Cost stop} = \frac{AC}{BC} = \frac{\text{Crash cost - Normal cost}}{\text{Normal time - Crash time}}$$

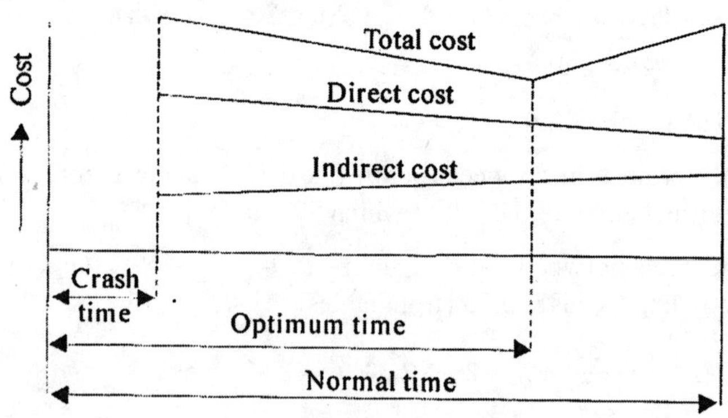

Time Cost – Trade off

Total Cost: The total cost of a project is the sum of Direct cost and Indirect cost.

The direct cost decreases with time

The indirect cost increases with time

Crashing of Project

Following steps are taken

Step – 1: Critical path – Draw the network diagram and find the critical path.

Step - 2: Find out the normal cost by adding all normal activity cost.

Step – 3: Calculate the cost slope of all the activities.

Step – 4: Crash the activities in the critical with minimum cost slope. Calculate the cost.

Step – 5: As the critical path duration is reduced, other path also become critical. So in order to reduce further parallel path are also to be reduced.

Step - 6: Crashing as per step 4 and 5 one reaches a point where further crashing increases the total cost. We have reached the optimum point.

Ex: A project has 7 activities. The normal time crash time, normal cost, crash cost of all activities are given. The fixed cost is Rs. 300 per day. Find the least cost duration of the project.

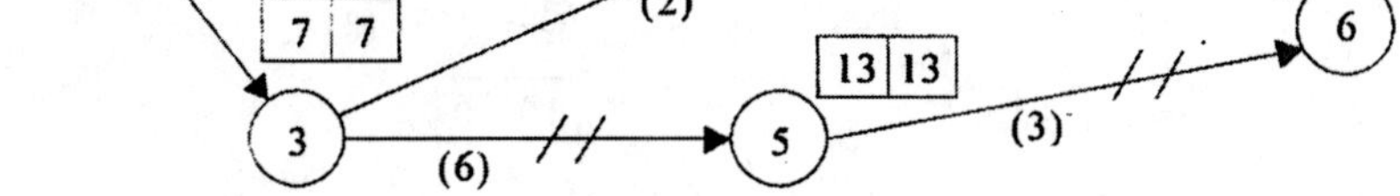

Total cost = 10600+16 x 300 = 15400

Calculation of cost slope

Or Cost of Crashing/day $\frac{\text{Crash cost} - \text{Normal cost}}{\text{Normal time} - \text{Crash time}}$

For activity $1 - 2 = \frac{1200 - 1000}{5 - 4} = 200/\text{day}$

1st Stage

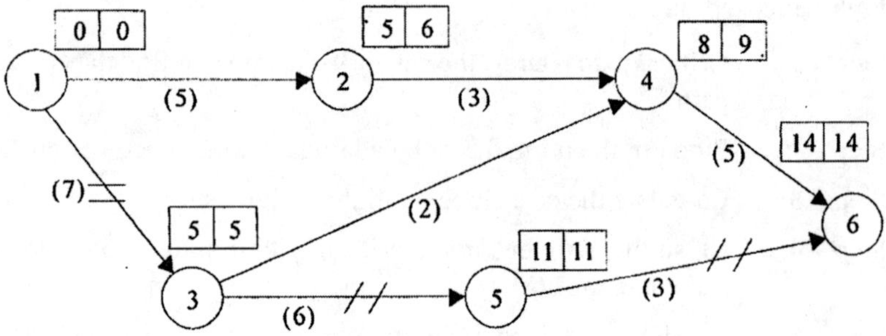

Direct Cost	=	10600	Indirect Cost	=	4800
Add		200	Add		600
		10800			4200

Total Cost =10800 + 4200 = 15000

2nd Stage

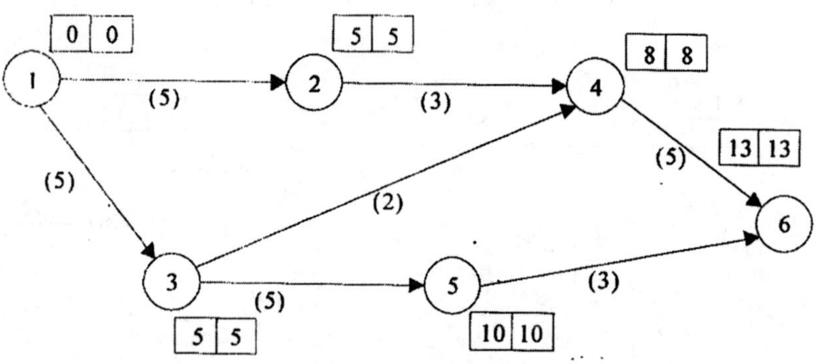

Crash 3 – 5 by 1 day

Direct Cost	=	1080	Indirect Cost	=	4200
Add		100	Add		100
		10900			3900

Total Cost = 10900 + 3900 = 14800

3rd Stage

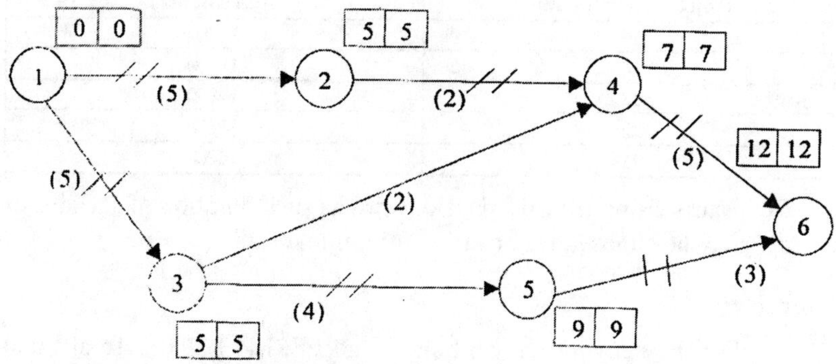

Crash 2 – 4 by 1 cost increase by Rs. 200

Crash 3 – 5 by 1 cost increase by Rs. 100

Direct Cost	=	10900	Indirect Cost	=	3900
Add		300	Less for 1 day		300
		11200			3600

Total Cost = 11200 + 3600 = 14800

4th Stage

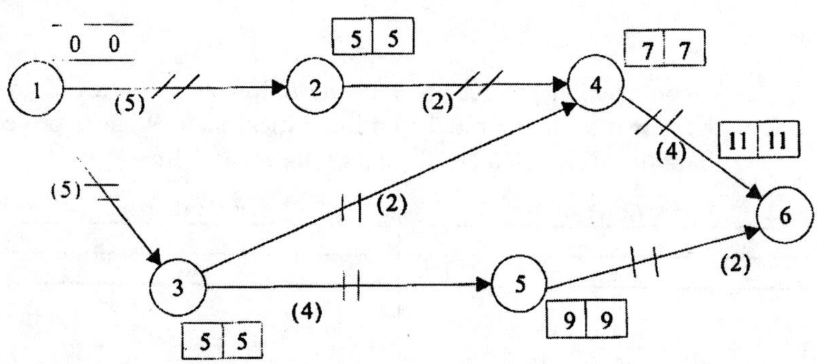

Crash	4 – 6 by 1 day	Cost increases by	Rs. 500
	5 – 6 by 1 day	Cost increases by	Rs. 200
			Rs. 700

Direct Cost	=	11200	Indirect Cost	=	3600
Add		700	Less for 1 day		300
		11900			3300

Total Cost = 11900 + 3300 = 15200

Summary

Project Duration (days)	Total cost (Rs.)
16	15400
14	15000
13	14800
12	14800
11	15200

Cost starts rising from 11 days onward as such duration of 12 days or 13 days may be choosen for ensuring minimum cost.

Exercise

1. For the network shown below find ES, EF, LS, LF, Total Float (TF), Free Float (FF), Independent Float (IF).

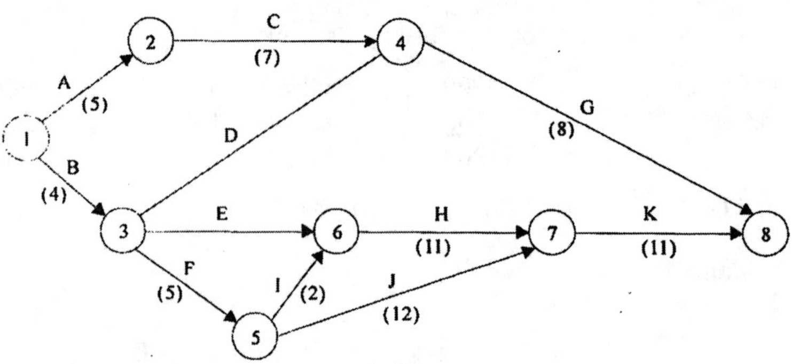

2. A construction project involves the following activities. Drawn the network diagram and find the critical path. What is project duration? Also calculate TF and FF for all activities.

Activity	Duration in days
1-2	3
1-3	16
2-4	5
3-4	Dummy
3-5	4
4-6	8
5-6	4
6-7	17
5-7	11

Resource Leveling

Ex. : A project has 7 activities. The relationship between the activities is as under:

Activity	A	B	C	D	E	F	G
Proceeding Activities				A	B	C	D

The duration of these activities and labour requirement for the activities are as under:

	A	B	C	D	E	F	G
Duration (week)	1	2	2	1	3	2	1
Labour requirement	2	1	1	1	1	1	1

The project duration should not exceed beyond the minimum project schedule. Only three men are available for the project execution. Find the resource schedule with respect to labour.

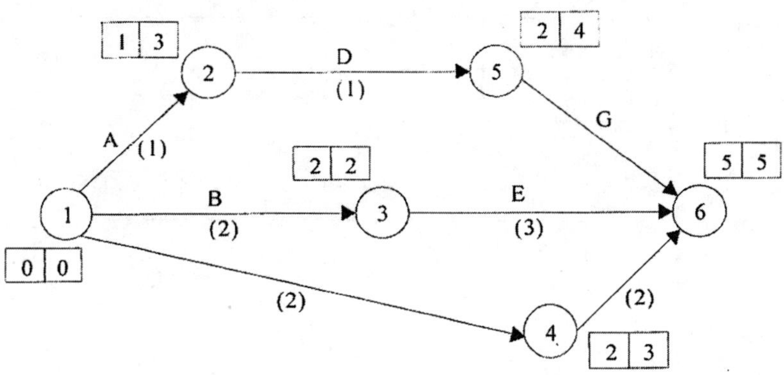

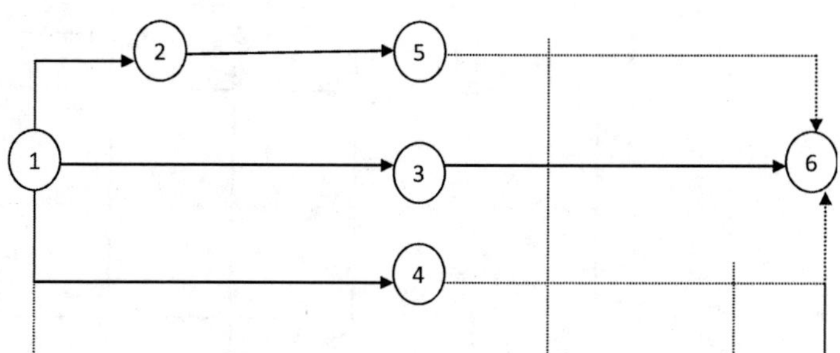

Week	1	2	3	4	5
Labour Requirement	4	3	3	2	1

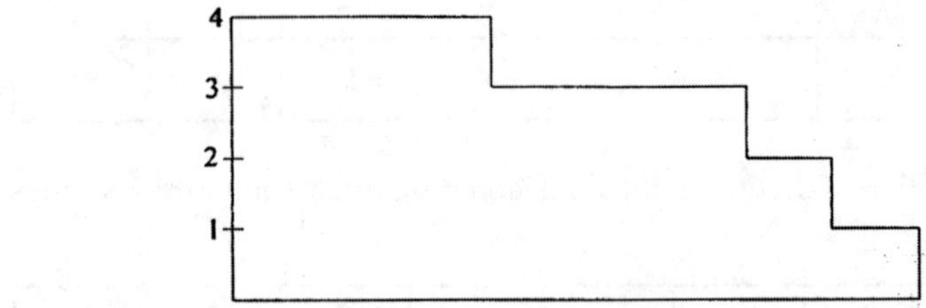

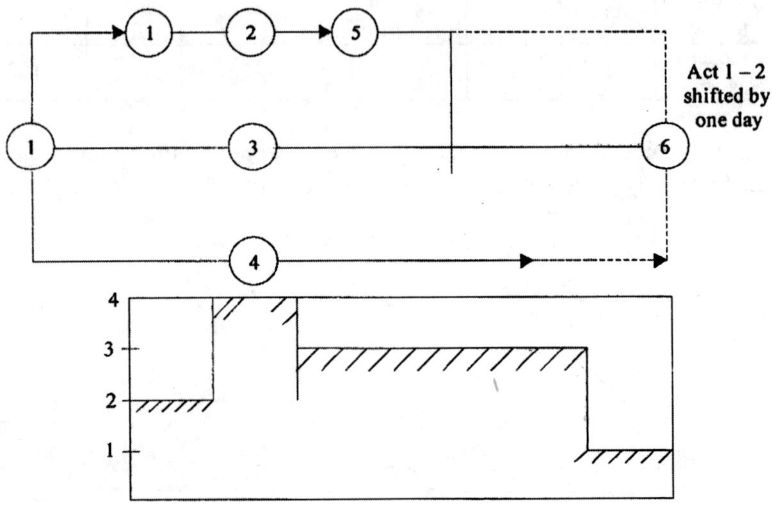
Act 1 – 2
shifted by
one day

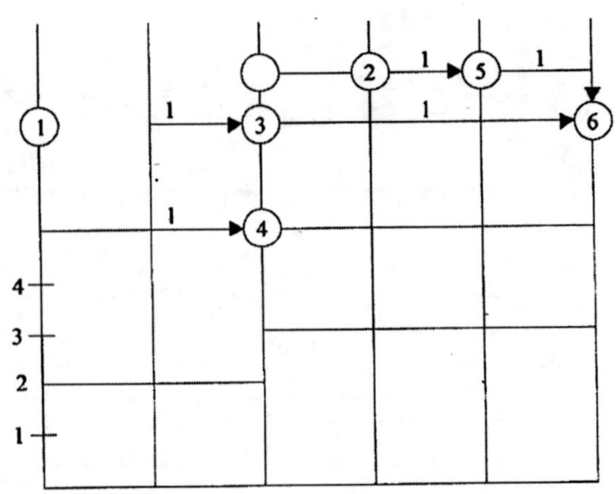

6.2 Project Direction and Co-Ordination

Project Direction – It refers to the use of authority to Channel's the activities of project on desired line.

Direction During start up phase

1. Scope of work
2. Schedule of work
3. Budget for work
4. System and procedures for work

These are done through project Kick-Off meeting. Following are achieved

1. Co-ordination of different agencies
2. Establishing control procedures
3. Team building
4. Information system

Direction for Design Review

Direction for Purchase Order

Direction during actual work

A project will require continuous direction till completion. If system and procedures work well then directions will be required only when problem occurs or unforeseen events occurs. In either case a decision has to be made as to what is to direction are part of everyday function of any manager.

This is done through project Review Meeting Following are discussed:

1. Status of implementation of decisions taken in earlier meeting
2. Progress achieved during the review period
3. Problems
4. Decisions regarding problem
5. Agreed action programmers

Project engineer, Vendor, Contractors could all be participants

Co-ordination – done through co-ordination meeting at all levels

6.3 Project Control –Along with direct project control has to be done project Control Comprises of

1. Project progress and Schedule control
2. Cost estimation and Cost Control

1. Project Progress and Schedule Control

This is done in three stages:

(a) Progress Control – This control has to be exercised almost daily at the operating level.

(b) Preventing schedule control – This control can be exercised at the project manager's level almost on daily basis.

(c) Predictive schedule control – This control is exercised both at project manager's level and also at the corporate management level.

2. Cost Estimation and Cost Control

There are following type of estimates are made

1. Order of magnitude estimate
2. Study estimate
3. Preliminary estimate
4. Definitive estimate
5. Detailed estimate

6.3.1 Order of magnitude Estimate

This estimate is made when a project has been identified and the entrepreneur wants to get a rough idea of the investment so as to decide whether to pursue that project or no.

(a) Investment pre annual tone capacity

If installed cost of plan pt of capacity C1 tone is Rupees R1 then installed cost R2 of plant P2 having annual capacity C2 can be estimated

$$R2 = \frac{R1 \times C2}{C1}$$

(b) Turn Over Ratio and Capital Ratio

The ratio between annual sales and investment expressed in rupees is known as Turnover ratio. The reverse of this i.e. the ratio between plant investment and annuals sales is known as capital ratio. If the capital ratio relating to a particular process and plant size is 'C' then for the proposed plant knowing the sales volume and price, the installed cost R2 can the estimated as R2= C x VI x P1 where V1 = annual sales volume.

(c) Six Tenth Factor

This a modification of the investment per annual tone capacity method. In this method plant investment is assumed to vary as 0.6 power of the size. Thus estimated cost R2 for the new plant can be computed as

$$R2 = R1x\left(\frac{C2}{C1}\right)^{0.6}$$

Where R1 and C1 represent the cost and capacity of a previously completed plant and C2 is the capacity of the proposed plant

(a) Inflation Index

The index is used in conjunction with methods (a) to (c) to correct investment figures to current cost

$$\text{installesd Cost (now)} = \text{Installedcost x } \frac{\text{Cost Index (new)}}{\text{Cost Index (Past)}}$$

Consumer price index as available from RBI Bulletin can be referred.

(b) Location Index

Knowing a plant cost in USA or in any other country, the cost of similar plant in India or any other country can be estimated using this index. The index can be developed if data related to productivity of countries involves is available.

The ratio methods are crude estimates and there may be error.

6.3.2 Study Estimate – This estimate is for studying the economic viability of the project. At this stage some more informations are available. Preliminary flow sheets, listing of major process equipment giving sizes and materials of construction are obtained from the process licensor. The accuracy at this stage is 1 30% since a project is approved on this estimate; the project authorities count cost over run on this estimate.

6.3.3 Preliminary Estimate – There is an urgent need to improve accuracy of cost estimate keeping this requirement in vies, cost estimates are made successively whenever adequate information, which will ensure further accuracy, is available. At this stage budget allocation is frozen and a basis of control is established. Accuracy at this stage is $\pm$ 20%.

6.3.4 Definite Cost Estimate – The estimate is prepared when the detailed engineering of a project is in advanced stage. Some more additional informations are available. These are:

1. Equipment purchase specification /vendor quotations/ awarded cost

2. Schedule of item for works tenders contractor's quotes / awarded cost.
3. Reasonably accurate material takes offs for steel, piping and electrical equipment based on general arrangement drawing.

   Accuracy is + 10%.

6.3.4 Detailed Estimate – This estimate is made on completion of engineering, ordering of equipment and machinery and award of field contract.

It cannot be more accurate since it cannot cover the construction phase.

Summary

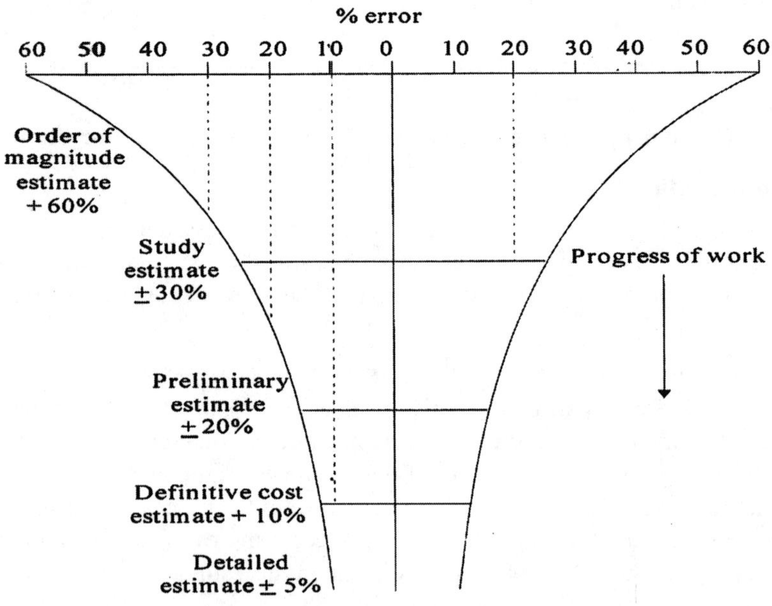

Various types of Estimates

6.3.5 Cost Control – The different methods that can be use different stages of project for cost control are given below.

1. **At zero data :** On the basis of the finalized basis package on itemized control estimate is prepared. Using the network plans, the control estimate is converted into cash flow plan and annually / quarterly budget. The control estimate and budget provides onward control of commitment and expenditure.

2. **During detailed Engineering :** The control estimate prepared before the zero date will be very soon overrun unless design and engineering procedure are constantly reviewed. Value engineering review should be carried out during the plowing stage of engineering development.

   (a) **Overall plot plan:** A review of plot plan can reduce, piping, cabling, roads drains, grading, paving and material land ling costs considerately.

   (b) **Specification of Plant and machinery:** A critical review of the functions of plant machinery will identify features or components that do not contribute to value. Further capacity balancing and design optimization would bring down plant and machinery cost the desired level.

   (c) **Utility System Design:** The size of the utility system and their location should be thoroughly reviewed. Consumption of utility per unit of output should be critically examined and optimization studies must be carried out on the same. Also the unity should be so located that piping and cabling costs become minimum.

   (d) **Building Design:** The number and size of building should be thoroughly examined for reduction cost.

   (e) **Standard specification and drawing:** Control should made on the on the not of drawings.

3. During procurement and sub-Contracting:

   (a) **Vender Association in specification:** if the specification requires item which are not in the standard range of manufacture the vendor will charge disproportionately extra cost. This can be avoided the designer is aware of market or the vendor is associated in preparation of the specification.

   (b) **Detailed scope and specification:** Preparation of detailed specification taken time and the vendor may also ask for more time for reading the same. However detailed specification will save a lot of extra claim, protracted negotiation and consequential delays that may inevitably take place after the placement of an order. Besides, if the details are known, the vendor will include unnecessary contingencies in the offer.

   (c) **General Conditions of contract:** The GCC should be reviewed in each care for affecting cost reduction.

(d) **Purchase Procedure:** The purchase procedure invariable increases the cycle time and hence the cost or purchase. Reduction in purchase cycle time will ensure reduction in price quoted by vendors.

(e) **Delivery in erectable sequence:** Unless equipment delivered to site can go directly to the foundation, money will be unnecessarily licked up without adding to the progress of the project. Also non sequential delivery or equipment and material will extend the project completion period there by adding to the cost of the project.

(f) **Competitive Bidding:** When qualified parties are asked to submit priced offers against detailed specification, due to competition least cost offers are likely to be submitted. This enables the reduction in the cost of equipment purchased. However, the bidders should be asked to submit their offers in structured format so that the bid can be evaluated properly. The price break up can also be used as the basis for discount should the price of an item appears higher than the others or the in housed estimate.

4. **During Construction:** There is not much scope for cost reduction during construction. However, there are certain items, as listed below, on which control must be exercised for keeping cost down.

(a) **Extra Items:** Efforts should be made to reduce the extras and negotiate their before taking up there items.

(b) **Idle Charges:** Release of drawing and work front to the contractor must be continuously monitored and necessary action taken to ensure that the contractor has always adequate work front to meet his contractual progress commitments the work of the various agencies also has to be well co-ordinate to ensure that no held up occurs in one contractor's work because of ineptly contractor. Supply of free issue materials like cement and steel. Must be planned in such a manner that speed of work does not suffer due to shortage of inputs.

(c) **Inventory Costs:** Purchase of bulk material should be carefully planned to ensure that there is no stock out and at the same time the inventory carrying cost in minimum.

(d) **Cash flow planning:** Fund shortage will not only slow down work but also attract additional cost. Over provision of fund will unnecessarily keep fund idling, two, resulting in excessive interest burden.